Key Stage 1 REVISE PRACTICE & HOME LEARNING

Writing & Handwriting

NAPE National Association for Primary Education

Contents

AUTHOR: Camilla de la Bédoyère
EDITORIAL: John Cattermole, Vicky Garrard, Julia Rolf
DESIGN: Jen Bishop, Dave Jones
ILLUSTRATORS: Bridget Dowty, Sarah Wimperis
PRODUCTION: Chris Herbert, Claire Walker

COMMISSIONING EDITOR: Polly Willis
PUBLISHER AND CREATIVE DIRECTOR: Nick Wells

3 Book Pack ISBN 1-84451-086-7   Book ISBN 1-84451-022-0
6 Book Pack ISBN 1-84451-089-1   Book ISBN 1-84451-095-6

First published in 2004

A copy of the CIP data for this book is available from the British Library upon request.

Created and produced by
FLAME TREE PUBLISHING
Crabtree Hall,
Crabtree Lane,
Fulham, London SW6 6TY
United Kingdom
www.flametreepublishing.com

Flame Tree Publishing is part of The Foundry Creative Media Co. Ltd.

© The Foundry Creative Media Co. Ltd, 2004

Printed in Croatia

Foreword

Sometimes when I am crossing the playground on my way to visit a primary school I pass young children playing at schools. There is always a stern authoritarian little teacher at the front laying down the law to the unruly group of children in the pretend class. This puzzles me a little because the school I am visiting is very far from being like the children's play. Where do they get this Victorian view of what school is like? Perhaps it's handed down from generation to generation through the genes. Certainly they don't get it from their primary school. Teachers today are more often found alongside their pupils, who are learning by actually doing things for themselves, rather than merely listening and obeying instructions.

Busy children, interested and involved in their classroom reflect what we know about how they learn. Of course they learn from teachers but most of all they learn from their experience of life and their life is spent both in and out of school. Indeed, if we compare the impact upon children of even the finest schools and teachers, we find that three or four times as great an impact is made by the reality of children's lives outside the school. That reality has the parent at the all important centre. No adult can have so much impact, for good or ill, as the young child's mother or father.

This book, and others in the series, are founded on the sure belief that the great majority of parents want to help their children grow and learn and that teachers are keen to support them. The days when parents were kept at arm's length from schools are long gone and over the years we have moved well beyond the white line painted on the playground across which no parent must pass without an appointment. Now parents move freely in and out of schools and very often are found in the classrooms backing up the teachers. Both sides of the partnership know how important it is that children should be challenged and stimulated both in and out of school.

Perhaps the most vital part of this book is where parents and children are encouraged to develop activities beyond those offered on the page. The more the children explore and use the ideas and techniques we want them to learn, the more they will make new knowledge of their very own. It's not just getting the right answer, it's growing as a person through gaining skill in action and not only in books. The best way to learn is to live.

I remember reading a story to a group of nine year old boys. The story was about soldiers and of course the boys, bloodthirsty as ever, were hanging on my every word. I came to the word khaki and I asked the group "What colour is khaki?" One boy was quick to answer. "Silver" he said, "It's silver." "Silver? I queried. "Yes," he said with absolute confidence, "silver, my Dad's car key is silver." Now I reckon I'm a pretty good teller of stories to children but when it came down to it, all my dramatic reading of a gripping story gave way immediately to the power of the boy's experience of life. That meant so much more to him, as it does to all children.

JOHN COE
General Secretary, National Association for Primary Education (NAPE).

Parents and teachers work together in NAPE to improve the quality of learning and teaching in primary schools. We campaign hard for a better deal for children at the vital early stage of their education upon which later success depends. We are always pleased to hear from parents.

NAPE, Moulton College, Moulton, Northampton, NN3 7RR,
Telephone: 01604 647 646 Web: www. nape.org.uk

Writing & Handwriting is one of six books in the **Revision, Practice & Home Learning** series for Key Stage One. These books have been devised to help you support your child as they approach the end of Key Stage One, in Year Two. Many children will be required to undergo assessment in preparation for their move to Key Stage Two.

The book follows key topics of the National Literacy Strategy and it aims to set out the key skills covered at school. Your child can revise each topic then practise the skills by completing the questions. You should go through the book together; your child will need you on hand to guide them through each subject. There are **Activity** boxes which give your child activities or investigations to carry out once the book has been put away.

You will also find **Parents Start Here** boxes to give you extra information and guidance.

Before you begin any learning session with the book, ensure your child is relaxed and comfortable.

- Ensure they are sitting comfortably.

- Encourage a good writing grip and neat presentation.

- Give your child access to water; research suggests that children who drink water when they work are able to perform better.

- Keep a dictionary to hand so you can help your child check spellings and research definitions.

Do not attempt to complete too many pages in one sitting; children have short attention spans and you want the experience to remain pleasurable. Offer your child plenty of praise for the work they accomplish. Revising is most effective if completed in short chunks. Topics should be revisited regularly to develop long-term memory patterns; your child is revising these topics for life, not just exams.

There is a checklist at the end of the book; you can use this to show your child how they are progressing. You could introduce a reward system too; children benefit enormously from rewards and praise.

Most importantly, the time you spend together with this book should be enjoyable for both of you.

Parents Start Here...

Top Tip! Remember to give your child lots of praise – they will work so much better.

Correct posture is essential for good handwriting. Check your child is sitting properly, has the book at a slight angle and is not slouching.

Handwriting

Remember!

- Sit comfortably with your bottom in the back of your seat.
- Check your pencil is sharp and you are holding it properly.
- Keep your feet on the floor, or resting on a box.

Copy each letter starting at the dot:

a a b b c c d d e e f f

g g h h i i j j k k l l

m m n n o o p p q q r r

s s t t u u v v w w x x

y y z z

4

Copy the capital letters starting at the dot:

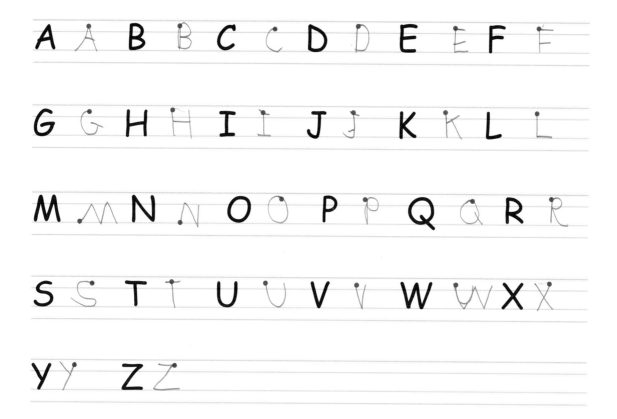

Activity

Stand up and stretch your arms up to the sky, as if you were climbing up a ladder. Swing your arms around like the sails of a windmill. This will help relax your muscles after all that hard work! You could also do this before you write as it will help you relax and think.

Check Your Progress!

Handwriting

Turn to page 48 and put a tick next to what you have just learned.

Parents Start Here...

Top Tip! Try and incorporate what your child learns into everyday life – they will remember it even better.

The National Literacy Strategy states that the tools used to teach children to read, such as letter patterns and phonics (sounds), should also be used to teach writing because the two activities are closely related.

Writing Simple Words

Remember!

- You can chop a word up into its sounds.

- Chopping words can help you to spell them.

- Writing a word out can help you learn how to spell it.

1. Read the whole passage. Choose the correct words to complete it:

~~jewels~~   ~~green~~   ~~men~~   ~~through~~   ~~Forest~~   ~~called~~

~~leaves~~   ~~money~~   poor

Robin Hood and his band of merry _men_ lived in Sherwood _Forest_. According to legend, their clothes were all coloured _green_. The men slept on piles of _leaves_. Robin Hood's girlfriend was _called_ Maid Marion. The band used to attack rich people travelling _through_ the wood. They stole _jewels_ and _money_ which they gave to _poor_ people living in the local village.

2. Write a vowel in the spaces here to make a word:

a e i o u

a) c_u_p

b) s_o_n

c) p_u_t

d) w_e_nt

e) th_a_t

3. a) Circle the words that have a y that makes the sound of the letter i saying its name. One has been done for you. Use a red pen or pencil:

(why) tidy happy my mostly

sky fly cry (nosey) crunchy try

b) The other words all have a y that makes the sound of the letter e. Circle them using a blue pen or pencil.

Activity

If you do not have a word book then now is the time to get one. You can write new words into it, spelling rules and the meanings of words.

Check Your Progress!
Writing Simple Words

Turn to page 48 and put a tick next to what you have just learned.

Top Tip!
Always look for positive aspects to your child's work as well as helping them to resolve errors.

Parents Start Here...

When your child is writing make sure they leave the correct spacing between words, sentences and paragraphs.

Sentences

Remember!

- A sentence is a group of words that tell you about something.

- A sentence begins with a capital letter.

- A sentence ends with a full stop.

1. Move the words around so the sentences make sense. Make sure you put in capital letters and full stops. The first one has been done for you:

a)   the the dog chased ball

The dog chased the ball.

b)   I the live countryside in _____

c)   things measure to used rulers are _____

d)   bike his broken is _____

e)   big have ears elephants _____

f)   on banana slipped I a _____

g)   ship hit the a rock sank and _____

2. Put the full stops into this passage:

When the Romans were in charge life was good They were very skilled at building towns and roads Roman children went to school and learned how to read, write and do sums I wish I had been born a Roman

3. Names also begin with capital letters. Write these sentences out, putting in all of the capital letters and full stops. The first one has been done for you:

a) when my cat, tom, died i cried and cried

When my cat, Tom, died I cried and cried.

b) some people believe that the story of cinderella is true

_____

c) the bakery is on wilton avenue

_____

d) i went to paris to visit my cousin henri

_____

Activity

Draw a picture of a Roman child. Use a book or the Internet to help you find out what Roman children wore.

Check Your Progress!

Sentences

Turn to page 48 and put a tick next to what you have just learned.

Top Tip! If your child loses concentration here, let them take a break.

Parents Start Here...

Being able to distinguish between objects and subjects will help your child understand the work of the verb in a sentence.

Nouns And Proper Nouns

Remember!

- Most sentences contain at least one noun.

- A noun is a word that names a thing, a place or a person, e.g. boy.

- A noun that names a particular thing, place or person is a proper noun, e.g. Stan.

- The noun that is doing something is called the subject of a sentence.

- A noun that is having something done to it is called the object of a sentence.

1. Underline the 9 nouns in this passage:

The witches danced around the fire. The tallest witch had a tall grey hat. The smallest witch had long blue fingernails. The fattest witch threw magic stones into the flames.

2. Circle the proper nouns. One has been done for you:

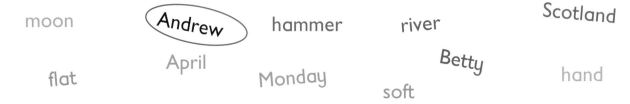

moon   Andrew   hammer   river   Scotland

flat   April   Monday   soft   Betty   hand

3. Draw a red circle around the subject in each sentence:

a) Asif touched the blanket.

b) The plane flew into the clouds.

c) Butterflies suck nectar.

Can you point to the object in each sentence?

4. Write sentences using these nouns:

a) crocodile _____

_____

b) jungle _____

_____

c) feathers _____

_____

TRY THIS **Activity**

Try to think of a sentence that does not contain any nouns.

Check Your Progress!
Nouns And Proper Nouns
Turn to page 48 and put a tick next to what you have just learned.

Parents Start Here...

Ask your child to identify the verbs in a story or non-fiction book they are reading.

Verbs

Remember!

- Most sentences have a verb.

- Verbs are doing words or being words.

- Doing verbs tell you about an action, e.g. kicking.

- Being verbs tell you how someone is feeling, e.g. hurting.

1. Write sentences using the verbs you are given here:

a) whisper _____

b) skating _____

c) smiling _____

2. Tick the verbs:

a) walk ☐   pavement ☐   lorry ☐   shoe ☐

b) camel ☐   roses ☐   smell ☐   tea ☐

c) cotton ☐   sew ☐   wool ☐   jumper ☐

3. Choose the correct verb to write into each sentence:

grow   wants   boiled   climbed

a) The thief _____ in through the open window.

b) Sammy _____ to eat ice-cream at the park.

c) The chef _____ the pot of potatoes.

d) Sunflowers can _____ to a height of 2 metres.

4. a) Tick the doing verb:

like ☐   climb ☐   feel ☐   want ☐

b) Tick the being verb:

looking ☐   liking ☐   running ☐   jumping ☐

TRY THIS

Activity

Write a list of as many verbs as you can. Which verbs are doing and which are being words?

Check Your Progress!

Verbs ☐

Turn to page 48 and put a tick next to what you have just learned.

Parents Start Here...

Letter patterns make particular sounds, known as phonics. Your child can use their knowledge of phonics to spell and read words.

Letter Patterns

Remember!

- Letter patterns make sounds.

- Letter patterns can help you spell new words.

- Learning new words will help your writing.

1. Choose a letter pattern to go in each word then write a sentence using the word:

ee   oa   oy   oo   ar   igh

a) m_____ting: _____

b) r_____st: _____

c) sh_____t: _____

d) ann_____: _____

e) br_____t: _____

f) st_____: _____

2. Write a sentence using the word star:

_____

_____

3. Add the letter pattern ing to each of these verbs and write the new word. One has been done for you:

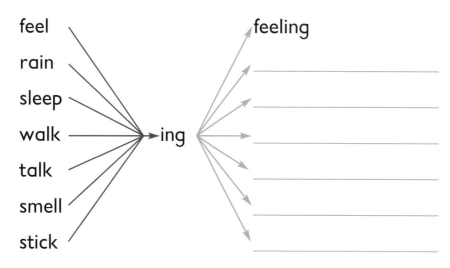

feel   feeling

rain

sleep

walk   ing

talk

smell

stick

4. Write a sentence using the word sleep:

_____

 Activity

Make your own wordsearch using words with these letter patterns. You will need to draw a box, put your words in, then add lots of different letters around them. Challenge a friend to find as many of the words as possible.

Check Your Progress!

Letter Patterns

Turn to page 48 and put a tick next to what you have just learned.

Parents Start Here...

Many writers are tempted to overuse the exclamation mark – and then it loses its power. Discourage your child from using it repeatedly in a piece of written work.

The Friends Of The Full Stop

Remember!

- Full stops show that a sentence is finished.

- Question marks ? and exclamation marks ! also mark the end of a sentence.

- Question marks show that a question is being asked.

- Exclamation marks are used to show pain, anger, surprise or danger.

- Commas , are used to show a break in a sentence, or in a list.

1. Write an exclamation mark in this box: ☐

   Write a question mark in this box: ☐

   Put a comma in this box: ☐

2. Use a question mark or an exclamation mark to finish each sentence:

   a) Stop doing that_____

   b) Where are you going_____

   c) How old are you_____

   d) That hurts_____

   e) Help me down_____

   f) Who is your best friend_____

16

3. Match the question to the answer. One has been done for you:

What time is it?   Fine, thanks!

What is your name?   I like green best.

What is your favourite colour?   We always go to Blackpool.

Where are you going on holiday?   About half past five.

How are you?   Jim, what's yours?

4. Put the commas into these lists. The first one has been done for you:

a) Bananas, apples, pears and grapes.

b) Cars lorries trains bikes and boats.

c) Red green orange and blue.

d) Socks shoes shorts shirts and slippers.

Activity

Play a game of 'Who Wants To Be A Winner?'. You will
need a watch or a clock, a notebook, pencil and blank paper.
Write lots of questions and their answers on the paper
(you may need to look in some non-fiction books for the
information). Now you are set to start your own quiz show...

> ### Check Your Progress!
> #### The Friends Of The Full Stop
> Turn to page 48 and put a tick next to what you have just learned.

Parents Start Here...

If your child finds it impossible to remember spellings, despite trying different techniques, they may have an underlying problem. Discuss this with your child's teacher.

Spelling

Remember!

- **Look** carefully at a word and find any letter patterns.

- **Chop** the word into sounds.

- **Write** the word in the air with your finger.

- **Cover** the word and write it down.

- **Check** your spelling and correct any mistakes.

1. Use the Look, Cover, Write method to learn these spellings:

Step One	Step Two	Step Three
Look at the word and learn it. Cover this list with paper.	Write the word down and check if it is correct. Cover.	Write the word again. Say the word.
camera		
kite		
light		
Monday		
bridge		
zebra		
white		
clouds		
mouse		

2. Cover the list of words and now use some of them to complete these sentences. No peeking!

a) We went to the zoo and saw a _____.

b) The Three Billy Goats Gruff wanted to cross a _____.

c) Let's go to the park and fly a _____.

d) The blue sky has white fluffy _____.

e) My favourite day is _____.

f) I took three photos with my _____.

g) I cannot sleep unless the _____ is on.

h) Mum found a dead _____ by the front door.

i) Some rabbits are brown, but my rabbit is _____.

TRY THIS

Activity

Learn how to spell the names of every day of the week. Wednesday is really tricky. Practise saying Wed-nes-day; you may find it helps.

Remember that the days of the week are written with capital letters.

Check Your Progress!

Spelling

Turn to page 48 and put a tick next to what you have just learned.

Top Tip! Remember to give your child lots of praise – they will work so much better.

Parents Start Here...

Talk to your child about the structure of the stories they are reading. Ask them what happened at the beginning and at the end, who the characters were, etc. Also ask them to predict what they think might happen next as you are reading – this develops their imaginative skills.

A Picture Story

Remember!

- Every story needs a beginning, a middle and an end.
- Sentences need to be clear and have the right punctuation.
- Take care with your spellings.
- Keep your handwriting neat.

Look at this picture story. Describe what happens in each picture. Draw a picture to show what happens in the end.

_____

_____

_____

_____

_____

_____

_____

_____

_____

_____

_____

 Activity

Use another piece of paper to draw a picture of your favourite character from a story you have read or that has been read to you.

Check Your Progress!

A Picture Story ☐

Turn to page 48 and put a tick next to what you have just learned.

21

Top Tip! If your child loses concentration here, let them take a break.

Parents Start Here...

Writing rhymes is the first step to writing poems. When you read poems to your child clap your hands to show the rhythm and meter.

Making Rhymes

Remember!

- Words that rhyme make the same sound.

- Poems often use rhyming words.

- When you are writing rhymes you must say the words aloud to hear the sounds.

1. Read this poem aloud:

> I had a little nut-tree, nothing would it bear
> But a silver nutmeg and a golden pear;
> The King of Spain's daughter came to visit me
> All for the sake of my little nut-tree.
> I skipped over water, I danced over sea,
> And all the birds in the air couldn't catch me.

a) Write the word that rhymes with bear: _____

b) Write the two words that rhyme with me: _____

c) What colour was the nutmeg? _____

d) What colour was the pear? _____

e) Who came to visit me? Write a sentence: _____

2. Join the words that rhyme. One has been done for you:

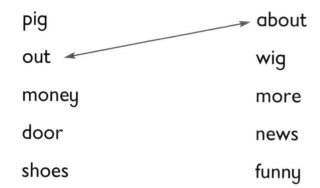

pig   about

out   wig

money   more

door   news

shoes   funny

3. Write three words that rhyme with seen:

_____

4. Complete this rhyme: Humpty Dumpty

Sat on a wall

Humpty Dumpty

Had a great _____ .

All the King's horses

And all the King's _____

Couldn't put Humpty

Together again.

Activity

Write out your favourite nursery rhyme on a separate piece of paper and decorate it with pictures.

Check Your Progress!

Making Rhymes ☐

Turn to page 48 and put a tick next to what you have just learned.

Top Tip!
Try and incorporate what your child learns into everyday life – they will remember it even better.

Parents Start Here...

Nouns, verbs and adjectives are all covered in Key Stage One but they are easily confused. Keep challenging your child to name the different parts of a sentence to ensure they are learnt and remembered.

Adjectives

Remember!

- Adjectives are describing words e.g. tall, fast, white and enormous.

- Adjectives describe nouns.

- Adjectives help us to make pictures using words.

- Adjectives make writing more interesting.

1. Circle the adjectives. There may be more than one in each sentence:

a) The grey whale swam beneath the waves.

b) A hungry caterpillar munched its way through the juicy apple.

c) A big dinosaur trampled on a little dinosaur.

d) Sharks are frightening.

2. Use these adjectives to finish the sentences:

broken   black   shiny   sour   wooden

a) The _____ table is a lovely brown colour.

b) The calm sea looked like a _____ mirror.

c) My calculator is _____ and it won't work now.

d) When the sky is _____ you can see the stars clearly.

e) The lemon was _____.

3. Write a sentence using the word beautiful:

_____

_____

4. Think of different adjectives to describe each of these nouns:

a) _____ bucket   b) _____ blanket

c) _____ boy   d) _____ monster

TRY THIS

Activity

Look in your reading book and find five verbs, five nouns and five adjectives.

Check Your Progress!

Adjectives ☐

Turn to page 48 and put a tick next to what you have just learned.

Top Tip!
Learning is fun, so if your child is tired, let them come back to this when they are fresh.

Parents Start Here...

Read the poem aloud to your child. The rhythm is like a train trundling along and the syllable pattern is 5-4-3. Clap your hands as you read to show your child the rhythm.

Presenting Your Work

Remember!

- Always use your best handwriting for stories and poems.

- Think about how your writing and pictures will fit on the page before you begin to write.

- Keep your pencil sharp.

- Underline your headings.

Mobile

Hi there. How are you?
Oh really? Good.
I'm fine too.

No, I'm on the train
I'm coming home,
Late again.

You're on a train too?
That's right it's the
6-oh-2.

I'm sat at the back.
No, get away,
Fancy that.

You say you can see
A woolly hat
Yeah – it's me!

Copy this poem in your best writing on the next page. You can decorate round the edge of your poem if you like.

_____

_____

_____

_____

_____

_____

_____

_____

_____

_____

_____

_____

Activity

Ask a grown-up to read a poem aloud to you and clap in time as they speak.

Check Your Progress!
Presenting Your Work ☐

Turn to page 48 and put a tick next to what you have just learned.

27

Top Tip! If your child struggles with anything, don't worry – let them go at their own pace.

Parents Start Here...

Long words can be daunting to young writers but chopping compound words into smaller words or sounds helps children tackle them with confidence.

Writing Long Words

Remember!

- Writing long words is easier if you chop them up into smaller words.

- Words you can chop are called compound words.

- You can chop other words into sounds.

- Sounds are called syllables.

- Use letter patterns to help you write long words.

1. Chop these compound words into smaller ones. The first one has been done for you:

a) butterfly ⟶ butter + fly

b) sandcastle ⟶ _____

c) fireworks ⟶ _____

d) clipboard ⟶ _____

e) sweetcorn ⟶ _____

f) grapefruit ⟶ _____

g) watermelon ⟶ _____

2. Copy this sentence using your best joined-up handwriting:

The postman rode the carthorse through the playground singing about dragonflies and doormats.

Did you notice 5 compound words that can be chopped into smaller words? Write two of them here:

3. Join these short words to make a new word. The first one has been done for you:

a) hand + writing   ⟶   handwriting

b) photo + copy   ⟶

c) lamp + shade   ⟶

Activity

Play Word Snap. Write down some compound words onto card then cut each one into two smaller words. Play snap with a friend; when the two halves come together to make a compound word you can shout 'snap'.

Check Your Progress!
Writing Long Words
Turn to page 48 and put a tick next to what you have just learned.

29

Top Tip!
Remember to give your child lots of praise – they will work so much better.

Parents Start Here...

Show your child the type of letters you receive. Let them see the difference between formal (business) letters and informal letters.

Writing A Letter

Remember!

- Letters can be to friends and family, or to people you don't know.
- Always use your best writing.
- Put your address in the top right hand corner.
- Write the other person's address on an envelope.

1. Write your friend's name and address on the envelope. Names and addresses begin with capital letters. You can draw a pretend stamp in the corner.

Draw a stamp here.

Start writing here.

2. Write a letter to a friend, telling them about your last holiday. Make your letter interesting by describing the things you saw or did.

Put your address here.

Put the date here.

Activity

Lots of letters get sent by email nowadays. If you have a computer, or know a grown-up with one, then ask them to help you send an email to someone you know.

Check Your Progress!

Writing A Letter ☐

Turn to page 48 and put a tick next to what you have just learned.

Top Tip!
If your child loses concentration here, let them take a break.

Parents Start Here...

Teach your child their address, telephone number and date of birth. We will look at this on the next page.

Words To Learn

Remember!

- You must know how to write the days of the week.

- You must know how to write the months of the year.

- Days of the week and months of the year start with capital letters.

1. Fill in the missing words:

a) The first month of the year is _____.

b) Christmas is always in the month of

_____.

c) My birthday is in _____.

d) My favourite month is _____

because _____.

2. a) Write your name here. Remember to use capital letters at the beginning of each name:

Forename: _____ Surname: _____

January

February

March

April

May

June

July

August

September

October

November

December

b) Do you have a nickname? If so, write it here:

Nickname: _____

3. Here are the days of the week. Copy them in your best handwriting. Remember to use capital letters:

Monday   _____

Tuesday   _____

Wednesday   _____

Thursday   _____

Friday   _____

Saturday   _____

Sunday   _____

4. Write today's date. Include the day, date, month and year:

_____

_____

TRY THIS

Activity

Cut out a piece of card for each member of your family. Draw a picture of each person on a card and write their name underneath.

Check Your Progress!

Words To Learn ☐

Turn to page 48 and put a tick next to what you have just learned.

Top Tip!
Always look for positive aspects to your child's work as well as helping them to resolve errors.

Parents Start Here...

Discourage your child from answering questions in words or phrases; they should be using complete sentences with accurate punctuation.

All About Me

Remember!

- You should know how to write your name, address and telephone number.

- Names should begin with capital letters.

1. Draw a picture of yourself here and complete the sentences:

a) My name is _____.

b) I live at _____.

c) My telephone number is _____.

d) My birthday is _____.

2. Answer these questions using sentences. Try to remember to use the right punctuation:

a) How many brothers and sisters do you have?

b) What are their names?

_____

c) What is your school called?

_____

d) What does your teacher look like?

_____

e) What is your favourite lesson?

_____

f) What is the name of your best friend?

_____

g) What do you like to do at playtime?

_____

h) What do you like to do after school?

_____

Activity

Ask your Mum or Dad what they liked best, or least, about school. Grown-ups love talking about the time when they were children!

Check Your Progress!

All About Me ☐

Turn to page 48 and put a tick next to what you have just learned.

Parents Start Here...

Some children have very vivid imaginations and find it easy to create characters, settings and plots. Children who have more difficulty can be prompted by suggestions like those given here.

Planning A Story

Remember!

- Before you write a story you need to plan it.

- Think about what is going to happen.

- Think about who the characters (people) are in the story.

- Decide where and when your story will happen.

- Make sure your story has an exciting beginning and strong ending.

- Use interesting words and descriptions.

- Jot all your ideas down before you begin.

1. Choose when the story will happen. Tick a box:

Ancient Rome ☐ the future ☐ yesterday ☐ Ancient Egypt ☐

2. Choose where the story will happen:

a house ☐ a castle ☐ a wood ☐ an island ☐

3. Choose a character:

an evil king ☐ a little boy ☐ a talking dog ☐ a princess ☐

4. Choose three adjectives from the ones here and circle them:

crumbling   wet   grey   old   rotten

shiny   wicked   dirty

5. You are going to write a story using all the words you have chosen. Use the space here to jot down some more notes about your story. Remember to think about what is going to happen. You will need to think of at least one more character and you can use as many other adjectives as you need to make the story come alive.

_____

_____

_____

_____

Write your story over the page and draw a picture of your main characters.

TRY THIS

Activity

Cut out interesting words from magazines and put them in a bowl. Pick out a handful of words and see how many of them you can use in a story.

Check Your Progress!

Planning A Story ☐

Turn to page 48 and put a tick next to what you have just learned.

My Story

Use these two pages to write your story and then draw a picture.
Remember to give your story a title.

(writing lines)

Check Your Progress!

My Story ☐

Turn to page 48 and put a tick next to what you have just learned.

Top Tip!
Learning is fun, so if your child is tired, let them come back to this when they are fresh.

Parents Start Here...

Creative writing allows a child to express themselves. When a child writes a poem they do not have to worry about a plot and they are free to write about their feelings and emotions. Praising your child's efforts will give them confidence and pleasure. They can never be wrong with a poem!

Writing A Poem

Remember!

- Poems may rhyme, but they don't have to.

- Poems sometimes tell a story.

- A poem may be about your thoughts and feelings.

Here is a poem written by a 7-year-old boy, Edmund Johnson. It is about his favourite animals.

Read the poem aloud.

Badgers

The badger's fur and the ragged forest

The badger's tongue and a doe's tear

The badger's foot and the stony ground

The badger's cold breath and icy wind

The badger's eye and the North Star

Badgers are so amazing.

Write a poem about your favourite animal. Remember that your poem, like Edmund's, does not have to rhyme.

Write your poem on a piece of scrap paper first, play with the words and change them if you like. Using your best writing copy it out below. Each new line of a poem starts with a capital letter.

You can decorate your poem with pictures of your favourite animal.

_____

_____

_____

_____

_____

_____

_____

 Activity

Start your own poetry book. You can write down all of your best poems.

Check Your Progress!

Writing A Poem ☐

Turn to page 48 and put a tick next to what you have just learned.

Top Tip! Try and incorporate what your child learns into everyday life – they will remember it even better.

Parents Start Here...

Show your child non-fiction reports, such as articles in the newspaper or magazines, or recipes in books.

Writing Non-Fiction

Remember!

- Non-fiction is writing that is not made-up, or imagined.

- Reports, recipes, instructions and stories about real people or events are all non-fiction.

- Non-fiction needs to be written with interesting words.

- Non-fiction writing needs to be planned, just like stories.

1. Describe your home. Remember to write in sentences and check your punctuation.

_____

_____

_____

2. Write a short report on the last school trip you went on, or the last day out you spent with your family.

_____

_____

_____

3. Describe a member of your family. Write about the way they look and the things they say or do.

4. Describe your favourite television programme, saying why you like it so much.

TRY THIS

Activity

Tell a grown-up about the things you would like to do during the next school holidays. Clearly explain what you want to do, and why.

Check Your Progress!
Writing Non-Fiction

Turn to page 48 and put a tick next to what you have just learned.

Parents Start Here...

Top Tip! Remember to give your child lots of praise – they will work so much better.

Children often forget that other people may not have the same knowledge, or information, as them. When your child writes instructions help them to include all the necessary details.

Writing Instructions

Remember!

- Instructions tell us what to do.

- Instructions are written in order.

- They may have pictures to help explain what they mean.

1. Imagine you meet a visitor at your school gate. He wants to know how to find your classroom. Write him some instructions. Remember to number the sentences:

_____

_____

_____

_____

_____

_____

2. An alien has come to stay with you. The alien is quite smelly because he has never seen water before. Write him some instructions explaining how he must keep himself clean. Remember to number the sentences:

_____

_____

_____

_____

_____

_____

_____

_____

_____

_____

(TRY THIS)

Activity

Ask a grown-up to show you some of the instruction booklets they have got for electronic equipment, like the television or video. You will notice that pictures are often used instead of words. Why do you think this is?

Check Your Progress!
Writing Instructions ☐
Turn to page 48 and put a tick next to what you have just learned.

Answers

Pages 6–7
1. Robin Hood and his band of merry <u>men</u> lived in Sherwood <u>Forest</u>. According to legend, their clothes were all coloured <u>green</u>. The men slept on piles of <u>leaves</u>. Robin Hood's girlfriend was <u>called</u> Maid Marion. The band used to attack rich people travelling <u>through</u> the wood. They stole <u>money</u> and <u>jewels</u> which they gave to <u>poor</u> people in the local village.
2. a) cap, cup
b) sin, sun
c) pet, pat, pit, pot, put
d) want, went
e) that
3. why, sky, fly, my, try and cry should all be circled in red.

Pages 8–9
1. b) I live in the countryside.
c) Rulers are used to measure things.
d) His bike is broken.
e) Elephants have big ears.
f) I slipped on a banana.
g) The ship hit a rock and sank.
2. When the Romans were in charge life was good. They were very skilled at building towns and roads. Roman children went to school and learned how to read, write and do sums.
I wish I had been born a Roman.
3. b) Some people believe that the story of Cinderella is true.
c) The bakery is on Wilton Avenue.
d) I went to Paris to visit my cousin Henri.

Pages 10–11
1. The <u>witches</u> danced around the fire. The tallest <u>witch</u> had a tall grey <u>hat</u>. The smallest <u>witch</u> had long blue <u>fingernails</u>. The fattest <u>witch</u> threw magic <u>stones</u> into the <u>flames</u>.
2. Andrew, Monday, Betty and Scotland are all proper nouns.
3. Asif, plane and butterflies are all subjects. Blanket, clouds and nectar are all objects.

Pages 12–13
2. a) walk
b) smell
c) sew
3. a) climbed
b) wants
c) boiled
d) grow
4. a) climb
b) liking

Pages 14–15
1. a) meeting
b) roast
c) shoot or sheet
d) annoy
e) bright
f) star
3. feeling
raining
sleeping
walking
talking
smelling
sticking

Pages 16–17
2. a) Stop doing that!
b) Where are you going?
c) How old are you?
d) That hurts!
e) Help me down!
f) Who is your best friend?
3. What time is it? About half past five.
What is your name? Jim, what's yours?
What is your favourite colour? I like green best.
Where are you going on holiday? We always go to Blackpool.
4. b) Cars, lorries, trains, bikes and boats.
c) Red, green, orange and blue.
d) Socks, shoes, shorts, shirts and slippers.

Pages 18–19
2. a) zebra
b) bridge
c) kite
d) clouds
e) Monday
f) camera
g) light
h) mouse
i) white

Pages 22–23
1. a) pear
b) tree and sea
c) silver
d) gold
e) The King of Spain's daughter came to visit me.
2. pig – wig
money – funny
door – more
shoes – news

3. clean, mean, bean, keen etc.
4. fall, men

Pages 24–25
1. a) grey
b) hungry, juicy
c) big, little
d) frightening
2. a) wooden or shiny
b) shiny
c) broken
d) black
e) sour

Pages 28–29
1. b) sand + castle
c) fire + works
d) clip + board
e) sweet + corn
f) grape + fruit
g) water + melon
2. The compound words are:
postman, carthorse, playground, dragonflies, doormats.
3. b) photocopy
c) lampshade

Pages 32–33
1. a) January
b) December

Check Your Progress!

Handwriting .... ☐

Writing Simple Words .... ☐

Sentences .... ☐

Nouns And Proper Nouns .... ☐

Verbs .... ☐

Letter Patterns .... ☐

The Friends Of The Full Stop .... ☐

Spelling .... ☐

A Picture Story .... ☐

Making Rhymes .... ☐

Adjectives .... ☐

Presenting Your Work .... ☐

Writing Long Words .... ☐

Writing A Letter .... ☐

Words To Learn .... ☐

All About Me .... ☐

Planning A Story .... ☐

My Story .... ☐

Writing A Poem .... ☐

Writing Non-Fiction .... ☐

Writing Instructions .... ☐